Finland
Air Forces
From Neutral to NATO

KEVIN WRIGHT

AIR FORCES SERIES, VOLUME 6

Front cover image: Finland's F/A-18 fleet, which has excelled in operating through the long cold Arctic winters will have served for more than 30 years before the F-35A replaces it. (Ilmavoimat)

Title page image: In 2007, the Finnish Air Force received 18 former Swiss Air Force Hawk Mk 66s. They have retained their distinctive red and white paint scheme. During 2023 they will all be gradually repainted in the standard grey scheme of other Ilmavoimat Hawks. (Kevin Wright)

Contents page image: The F/A-18 has provided the Ilmavoimat's main combat power since late 1990, a formidable air-defence fighter and packing an impressive punch as a ground-attack aircraft. (Sebastian Viinikainen)

Acknowledgements

I would like to offer grateful thanks to the Finnish Air Force Media Service for its help with images and to the following who very kindly allowed me to use their images for this book: Stefan Wright-Cole, Sami Niemeläinen, Sebastian Viinikainen, Juha Ritaranta, Mark Salter, Mike Butorac, Gerard van der Schaaf, Patria, the Swedish Armed Forces and Finnish Army.

Kevin Wright

Published by Key Books
An imprint of Key Publishing Ltd
PO Box 100
Stamford
Lincs PE9 1XQ

www.keypublishing.com

Typeset by SJmagic DESIGN SERVICES, India.

Contents

Chapter 1   Forged in War 4

Chapter 2   Peacetime Cadre 10

Chapter 3   Flying Training 16

Chapter 4   Hornet Power 25

Chapter 5   From 'HX' to F-35 39

Chapter 6   Transport and Intelligence 45

Chapter 7   Wartime and Dispersed Operations 56

Chapter 8   Finnish Army and Border Control Aircraft 74

Chapter 9   From Neutral to NATO 84

Chapter 1

Forged in War

Long associated with neutrality, Finland came into being in 1918 in the wake of the Russian Revolution. Ever since then the Finnish Defence Forces (Puolustusvoimat) have played a major role in maintaining the country's security and territorial integrity. Throughout the last century of the country's existence, it is the relationship with its giant neighbour Russia with which it shares a 1,340km/830-mile long land border that has been most problematic. The relationship is often tense; in November 1939 Finland was subjected to existential threat when it was invaded by the USSR. Ever since, Russia has remained at the heart of Finland's security concerns.

The Finnish Air Force (Ilmavoimat) was formed on 6 March 1918, when it received its first aircraft – a Thulin Type D reconnaissance aircraft. This date is celebrated as marking the foundation of the Finnish Air Force. It was a gift from Swedish Count Eric von Rosen, and featured the Count's personal good luck symbol of a right-facing blue swastika painted on its wings. This was subsequently adopted as the Finnish Air Force's national insignia until 1945.

During the 1920s, Air Force procurement focused mostly on small numbers of varying types. In the 1930s, as war approached, the Air Force operated Fokker D.XXI fighters and Fokker C.X scout and light bombers from the Netherlands, some 18 Bristol Blenheims and a number of obsolete Bristol Bulldogs from Britain. Later additional overseas 'donations' included more than 137 mixed Fokkers, some 97 Blenheims and 19 Bulldogs.

However, the Ilmavoimat came of age in the Winter War that began with a Soviet invasion on 30 November 1939. At the outbreak of war, the 100-aircraft strong Finnish Air Force was at a severe numerical disadvantage, heavily outnumbered, and concentrated on air defence and reconnaissance operations. By the time this 105-day war came to an end, the Ilmavoimat's situation had begun to improve significantly, following the arrival of numerous aircraft purchases including 44 Brewster

A Thulin Type D reconnaissance aircraft gifted from Swedish Count Eric von Rosen on 6 March 1918 marked the foundation of the Ilmavoimat (Finnish Air Force). (SA-kuva)

The British government donated Blenheims to the Finnish Air Force, with another 55 built under licence by the Finnish State Aircraft Factory. (SA-kuva)

Model 239s, 35 Fiat G50s and 13 Hawker Hurricanes, plus foreign donations including 87 Morane Saulnier MS 406 fighters. Another 30 Soviet aircraft were captured more or less intact. During the conflict, the Finnish Air Force recorded more than 300 aerial victories and lost 62 of its own aircraft (47 to enemy fire) and another 35 damaged. In total, 75 members of the Air Force were killed or reported missing in action. Finnish anti-aircraft defences also brought down a large number of enemy aircraft. Although the fighting ended on 13 March 1940, Finland was forced to cede territory (part of eastern Karelia, Salla and Petsamo) to the USSR in a subsequent peace treaty.

Following the end of the Winter War, the Air Force's capabilities significantly improved. Germany, seeing Finland as a potential ally against the USSR, quickly built closer relations with the country. By mid-1941, the Finnish Air Force had more than 550 aircraft, including a few dozen Curtis 75s captured by the Germans in France and Norway, and donated to Finland. Combat with Russia resumed on 22 June 1941 when German units stationed in Finland attacked Soviet forces in Operation Barbarossa. Ilmavoimat units soon engaged in operations to repulse Soviet air attacks. The Brewster Buffalo achieved particular success with the Finns, claiming 459 kills for the loss of 15 aircraft. These were

The Brewster Buffalo achieved particular success with the Ilmavoimat, claiming 459 kills for the loss of just 15 aircraft. (SA-kuva)

subsequently replaced by 159 German Messerschmitt Bf109s with Finnish bomber forces also receiving 15 German DO 17s and 24 JU 88s. Captured Soviet aircraft were also pressed into use. As the war turned against Germany, intermittent peace negotiations between Finland, the USSR and Western allies, saw an armistice agreement reached that brought an end to the 'Continuation War' in September 1944. The following month, after the Soviets applied pressure, the Finns committed to fight the Germans and they mounted their final battles of the war in what became known as the 'Lapland War' against the crumbling Luftwaffe forces in Northern Finland.

By the time that war ended in April 1945, the 'special detachment' that the Ilmavoimat had committed to the war reported 10 aircraft lost from an original strength of 60, with 16 crew killed and two captured. The final Finnish Air Force sortie in the Lapland War was flown by a DO 17 on a photographic reconnaissance mission on 4 April 1945.

Post-war treaties required Finland to make financial reparations and permanently cede territory to the USSR. The long-term effect for the rest of the Cold War was that Finland remained partially detached from Western Europe and in the shadow of Soviet power. The subsequent 1947 Paris Peace Treaty and the 1948 'Agreement of Friendship, Cooperation, and Mutual Assistance' with the Soviet Union gave it significant influence over Finnish political affairs. Within the 1947 treaty, restrictions were imposed on the Finnish military that included clauses specifying that the Air Force should have no more than 60 combat aircraft and was prohibited atomic weapons. The Ilmavoimat's manpower strength was fixed at a maximum of 3,000 people and the holding of 'offensive weapons' was forbidden. Later, the rules on possession of guided missiles and having a few bombers (to be used as target tugs) were eased. At that time, the Air Force possessed around 100 heavily used Messerschmitt Bf 109s as its main equipment, the last eventually retired in 1954. It was at this time that the swastika symbol was replaced

Left: The Ilmavoimat received 15 DO 17s from Germany, the type flying the last Finnish sortie of the Lapland War on 4 April 1945. (SA-kuva)

Below: The Ilmavoimat received 159 Messerschmitt Bf 109s; the last few only retired in 1954. (SA-kuva)

on Finnish aircraft with the familiar blue-and-white roundels used today. However, the swastika symbol remained on a few unit badges and in Air Force heraldry until it was quietly removed in 2020.

Even with treaty constraints in place, Finland took territorial defence of its borders very seriously acquiring 15 de Havilland Vampires, which entered service in 1954, followed by 13 Folland Gnats from 1958. Finland also purchased 80 two-seat Fouga Magisters, the first 18 arrived in 1958 with another 62 built under licence by Valmet. Like its successor, the BAE Hawk, the Magisters were two-seat machines, counted as training aircraft. Thus they were not included in the 64-combat aircraft ceiling, despite having a combat capability. During the Cold War, Finnish purchases of combat aircraft were

De Havilland T.55 Vampire from the Norwegian Air Force Historical Squadron, briefly wearing Finnish markings in 2013. The Ilmavoimat purchased nine T.55s Vampires in 1955. (Sami Niemeläinen)

Counted as a training aircraft, the Fouga Magister was able to side-step post-war restrictions on the number of combat aircraft the Ilmavoimat could operate. (Kevin Wright)

split between both East and West. In total, 48 Swedish Drakens of all variants eventually flew with the Ilmavoimat, including 12 assembled from kits supplied locally by Valmet. The first was delivered in 1974 with the final retirements in 2000. From the USSR, 13 MiG-21F-13s initially operated in fighter roles from 1973 until 1986. Nine more were added between 1984 and 1986 for reconnaissance work. From 1978 26 MiG-21bis arrived and operated until they were withdrawn in 1998. A total of six two-seat MiG-21s (two U and four UM variants) eventually served with the Finnish Air Force.

It was only after the collapse of the USSR in 1991 that Finland moved out of Russia's shadow. Despite having a generally strong, advanced economy, benefiting from advantageous trade relations with the USSR during the Cold War, following the Soviet collapse Finland suffered a deep recession. 'Escape' from Russia's economic orbit was cemented in 1995 when Finland joined the European Union and became fully anchored to Western institutions. In foreign policy terms, although deferential to the USSR, Finland took an overtly neutral stance, although firmly westward looking. After the Soviet collapse, Finland almost exclusively purchased Western equipment, with the biggest deal in 1992 being the purchase of the F-18 Hornet to replace its old MiG-21s and Draken fighters.

Left: Fouga Magisters continue to fly over Finland, with two aircraft operated by the 'Silver Jets' team. (Kevin Wright)

Below: Saab 35FS, DK-211 at Ivalo in May 1982, one of 48 Drakens operated by the Ilmavoimat up to 2000. (Juha Ritaranta)

In 1973, the Ilmavoimat received 13 MiG-21 F-13s from the USSR; these were retired in 1986. (Ilmavoimat)

26 MiG-21Bis were purchased by Finland and remained in service until 1998. Photographed at Helsinki-Vantaa airfield in 1983. (Juha Ritaranta)

Chapter 2

Peacetime Cadre

Today, Finland relies on a small professional military and has a strong tradition of conscription. Full wartime mobilisation can transform Finland's armed services into one of Europe's largest military forces with more than 280,000 personnel. In peacetime, the Finnish Defence Forces comprises a separate Army, Navy and Air Force. In wartime, a fourth service is added when the Finnish Border Guard comes under the control of the Defence Forces.

Force structure and conscription

The Ilmavoimat, like other Finnish Defence Forces, is built on a combination of professional, conscript and reserve forces, and on full wartime mobilisation reaches 38,000 personnel. During the Cold War public support for the conscription system fluctuated, hitting a low in the 1960s and 1970s. However, after 1989, public support for conscription increased at a time when most other European countries largely abandoned theirs as the Cold War ended. A constantly evolving conscription system, it took on a much greater significance after the 2014 Russian occupation of Crimea, increasing again after the start of the Russian invasion of Ukraine in February 2022.

When Finnish men turn 18 they are 'called-up'. Women apply for military service on a voluntary basis. A person's fitness for service is checked, their service preferences recorded and a service entry date is defined (with some deferments possible). The period of conscription lasts for either 165, 255 or 347 days based on the armed service and the position individuals are assigned to. The standard basic requirement is a minimum service of 165 days, while for those needing special skills the training period is 255 days. Conscripts who are training to become officers, non-commissioned officers, or training for the most specialized duties serve for 347 days. Approximately 43 percent of conscripts serve for 347 days, some 14 percent for 255 days, and 43 percent for 165 days.

When military service is complete, service personnel pass onto the reserve list where they remain until they are 50 years old, or 60, if they are officers or NCOs. Up to their age limit they can be called

New Ilmavoimat personnel from Karelian Air Command are sworn in at a ceremony at Rissala-Kuopio Air Base during summer 2022. (Ilmavoimat)

up for refresher training for a maximum of between 80 and 150 days, or 200 days for officers and NCOs (non-commissioned officers). Each year, about 18,000 reservists participate in mandatory training and 6,000 more take part in voluntary training. Most men, (not officers or NCOs) on reaching 50 years of age pass from the reserve pool to the 'auxiliary reserve' for another 10 years. This means there is a reserve pool of approximately 900,000 citizens, with the total armed forces wartime strength set at around 280,000 soldiers at any one time; the remainder of the reserve pool are available to local defence forces.

Air Force Command Finland (AFCOMFIN)

The Ilmavoimat consists of approximately 2,000 full-time uniformed and non-uniformed service members and it trains around 1,300 new conscripts each year. It is organised into three subordinate operational commands plus the Air Force Academy under the control of Air Force Command Finland (AFCOMFIN). Headed by a Major General, with a Brigadier General as Chief of Staff, AFCOMFIN is headquartered at Jyväskylä–Tikkakoski airfield, also home to the Air Force Academy. The Air Force maintains its own Administrative, Personnel, Operations, Plans, Logistics, and C4IS Divisions together with Flight Safety and Public Affairs. AFCOMFIN is responsible for coordination with the Army, Navy, Border Guard and other civilian authorities, and managing the Air Force's international cooperation.

A key element through which AFCOMFIN exercises its responsibilities is the Air Operations Centre, which is responsible for monitoring and securing Finland's air defences. It produces a real time 'recognised air picture' that is so vital for a modern integrated air defence system. Ilmavoimat's frontline air combat power is concentrated in two of its three geographical commands.

Lapland Air Command

Lapland Air Command (Lapin Lennosto) is situated at Rovaniemi Air Base inside the Arctic circle, just over 700km/435 miles north of Helsinki. One of the Ilmavoimat's main operating bases, it is responsible for the air defence of Northern Finland and home to the F/A-18C/D Hornets of Fighter Squadron 11 (Hävittäjälentolaivue 11, HävLLv 11) with its two component flights. It maintains aircraft on permanent QRA (quick reaction alert) for the air-policing mission, although numbers and readiness levels are undisclosed. Non-flying units include No 5 Control and Reporting Centre (CRC), which manages the radar units subordinated to it across the Lapland Air Command area, together with base support and maintenance facilities. Rovaniemi Air Base's staff is composed of approximately 350 military and 80 non-uniformed personnel. Lapland Air Command, like the other air commands, operates with a combination of full-time personnel, conscripts and reservists.

The basic period of military conscription for men is 165 days, with longer periods for those in command and technical positions. (Ilmavoimat)

Lapland's severe winter weather poses major challenges to mounting military operations, although the Finns are particularly well prepared. The Finnish Army's Lapland Jaeger Brigade, headquartered at Sodankylä, consists of two battalions: the Lapland Jaeger Battalion and the Rovaniemi Air Defence Battalion. The latter has two Air Defence Batteries and an Airbase Support Company. The units are mostly composed of conscripts trained within the Jaeger Brigade to operate Crotale NG anti-aircraft missiles and US Stinger MANPADS supplied in 2014. In 2006, Finland had received a large number of Russian SA-11 SAMs, as settlement of a Soviet-era debt. These were replaced with Norwegian NSAMS 2, selected in 2009 and known as the ITO 12 locally. A large number of 23 ITK 61 anti-aircraft guns and modernised 23 ITK 95s fitted with an aiming computer, thermal camera, and laser-range finder to enhance their accuracy, are also available to the service.

The Air Defence Batteries provide training for different elements of ground-based air defence equipment including their command, control and support systems. They also train the NCO cadre responsible for ground-based air defence. A special training programme covers the Jaeger Brigade's military police responsibilities, which include protecting the Rovaniemi and Sodankylä garrisons. The support and HQ platoons work with different types of specialised vehicles and logistics equipment. The Airbase Support Company trains personnel in logistics-related tasks, including those allocated to supply and transport platoons, paramedic and evacuation teams. It provides the training for aircraft maintenance conscripts, fuel specialists, mechanics, military drivers and UAV operators.

Left: The ITO90M Crotale missile purchased by Finland entered production in 1990. Operated by the regional air commands, this version has a 13kg/28lb warhead, an 11km/7-mile range and a 6000m/20,000ft ceiling. (Ilmavoimat)

Below: The formidable Norwegian NSAMS 2, known as the ITO 12, in Finnish service, was selected in 2009 to replace Finland's Soviet-era SA-11s that it had acquired a few years earlier. (Puolustusvoimat)

Above: On the firing range in 2016, Finland possesses 23 ITK 95 anti-aircraft guns used for local air defence. (Puolustusvoimat)

Right: The RBS 70 MANPAD is manufactured by Saab Bofors. Known as the ITO 05 1 in Finland, it can also be stand mounted and has a 5km/3-mile range. (Puolustusvoimat)

Karelia Air Command

Karelia Air Command's (Karjalan Lennosto) main operating base is at Rissala-Kuopio. Its area of responsibility covers the East and Southeastern parts of Finland and is composed of approximately 500 full-time personnel, with another 250 conscripts at any one time. Karelia Air Command is structured in a similar manner to its Lapland counterpart. Fighter Squadron 31 (HävLLv 31), is divided into two Flights as the Command's major combat component. It is responsible for No. 7 CRC (control and reporting centre) and the subsidiary military and civilian radars in its area of responsibility. Similarly, it has a Base Support Squadron, C4I and maintenance centres, and can utilise a PC-12NG communications aircraft for any necessary tasks.

The Salpausselkä Air Defence Battalion (Salpausselän Ilmatorjuntapatteristo, SALPITPSTO) with three air defence batteries (Ilmatorjuntapatteri), fulfil the same functions as its Lapland Air Command counterparts.

The PC-12NG entered Ilmavoimat service in 2010 and has proved to be a highly versatile light transport aircraft. (Mark Salter)

Satakunta Air Command

Satakunta is the third of the geographic air commands, covering Southwestern Finland, centred on Tampere-Pirkkala Air Base. Its responsibilities include a range of flying operations, plus some research and flight testing (including the development of air warfare doctrine and tactics). Prior to its disbandment in June 2014, HävLLv 21, equipped with F/A-18s, operated from Pirkkala after which its aircraft were redistributed to the two other Hornet units as part of a major armed forces reorganisation.

The flying element of the command comprises an HQ and four Operational Flights (Tukilentolaivue–TukiLLv). All are based at Tampere-Pirkkala: One Flight operates two of Finland's C295M aircraft in the transport role, Two Flight has three LJ35As, Three Flight uses the third Finnish C295M in the signals intelligence collection role, and Four Flight six PC-12NGs. A small number of F-18s have also been used for flight and weapons test tasks. The Command maintains No. 3 Control and Reporting Centre, an aircraft maintenance squadron, a logistics flight and has a force protection element. It has conscript and reservist training responsibilities as the other two Commands have.

The C295M has proved invaluable, utilised by all branches of the Defence Forces for medium transport tasks. (Ilmavoimat)

Air Force Academy

In addition to being the location for HQ AFCOMFIN, the Air Force Academy (Ilmasotakoulu) at Tikkakoski in Jyväskylä, is the hub of Ilmavoimat training and education. Given the large numbers of recruits conscripted annually and the regular training of reservists and regular forces, training activities are a major function for all Finland's armed forces. The Air Force Academy's training battalion is home to the Ilmavoimat Reserve Officer and NCO Training Schools, a Signal Technology Company and an Air Traffic Engineer Company. It provides specialized training for air defence ground operators (including SAM systems, radar surveillance and fighter controllers), aircraft maintenance, communications, force protection and military vehicle operators. Like other main operating bases, Jyväskylä–Tikkakoski has its own Base Support Squadron, C4I centre and maintenance facility

Most visibly, Jyväskylä–Tikkakoski is the central location for Finnish AF flight training. Basic flight training was undertaken from the 1970s using the indigenously produced L-70 Vinka aircraft, which were gradually replaced by Grob G115E-FIN aircraft that arrived in 2016. Flight training begins with a primary flight syllabus in which students follow the Pilot Reserve Officer Course. In the subsequent phase of training, students undertake studies on the pilot's programme at the National Defence University.

Advanced training is undertaken by Squadron 41 flying a mixture of BAE Hawk versions divided into three flights. The base is also home to the internationally famous 'Midnight Hawks' aerobatic team that displays across Europe, flown by Air Force Academy Hawk instructors.

Above: A small fleet of second-hand, updated Grob 'G115E-FIN' aircraft provide flight training for Ilmavoimat pilots. (Ilmavoimat)

Right: The Midnight Hawks is Finland's national aerobatic team, piloted by instructors from the Air Force Academy. (Mark Salter)

Chapter 3

Flying Training

A s in most modern Western air forces, competition to become an Ilmavoimat aircrew member is intense. After initial military training, those selected for aircrew progress to primary flight training. Until 2022, this was based on the domestically produced Valmet L-70 Vinka. The prototype 'LEKO-70' first flew in July 1975 and the first of 30 examples entered service with the Air Force at Kauhava Air Base in 1980, the final one in 1982.

The type provided basic training to nearly all military fixed and rotary wing pilots and those from the Finnish Border Guard. The Vinka gave pilots their first solo flights, provided cross country navigation, night, aerobatic and low visibility training, and was also regularly used as a liaison aircraft.

The aircraft received several modifications during its lifespan. Juhani Stenhäll, an aircraft engineer explained that the biggest changes were made in 2002, as the planes approached their 5,000-flight-

Left: The Valmet L-70 Vinka provided basic training for Finnish pilots from 1980 until 2022. (Ilmavoimat)

Below: In 2002, the L-70 Vinkas underwent an update programme that extended their service life by another 2,000 hours. (Sebastian Viinikainen)

hour limit. 'The major modifications involved the renewal and strengthening of the wing-fuselage attachments and the replacement of sheet metal frames in the aft fuselage.' These added another 2,000 hours to the L-70s service life. 'At the same time, we also modified the avionics and installed more modern displays.' These included a Garmin GNS 430 navigation and communications avionics fit. In 2005, the Pilot Reserve Officer Course, (through which trainee military pilots progress) and their Vinkas moved from Kauhava AB to Tikkakoski.

In 2005, Finnish defence company Patria (formerly Valmet) took over the provision of basic training in the Air Force with the Vinka and became responsible for the fleet. Joni Mahonen, a Patria flight instructor, was one of the final pilots to fly the L-70, accumulating 1,063 flight hours on the type. He first encountered it in 1989 when he started his own training. 'It was reliable and easy to fly. It was more forgiving of pilot error than many other planes and you could perform almost the full range of aerobatic manoeuvres with it, with the exception of tail slides.' It's robust fixed landing gear, able to withstand rougher touchdowns, was a major plus in training use. The last Vinka was retired on 31 August 2022 with some of the airframes passed to museums and engineering institutions, and the final 15 remaining aircraft auctioned off.

In 2005, Finnish defence company Patria took over responsibility for the delivery of basic training mainly using former Ilmavoimat instructors. (Sami Niemeläinen)

The last Vinka retired from service in August 2022, with some given to museums and others auctioned to civilian buyers. (Ilmavoimat)

Grob 115E

The Ilmavoimat took delivery of the first of its 28 second-hand Grob 115E/EA two-seat trainers in November 2016. Purchased from UK-based Babcock International for approximately 6.6 million Euros, the aircraft had previously served with the British military. The remaining airframes were delivered during 2017, but their subsequent use was piecemeal until a significant modification programme was implemented.

The first of the modified Grob G115E-FINs, completed by Patria, was flown by a student pilot from Tikkakoski on 24 January 2020. All 28 aircraft underwent a thorough airframe maintenance check and had a significant avionic systems update, including the installation of a modern glass cockpit. Cadet flight hours in the Grob comprise approximately 40 hours of elementary flight training and 50 flight hours for the advanced training syllabus, before progressing to the Hawk.

An important element of wider efforts to enhance Finnish Air Force flight training was the development of a more modern integrated simulator system. For the Grob 115s this meant a realistically representative cockpit and the ability to provide an effective 'Live, Virtual and Constructive' (LVC) training environment. The new 'GO' simulator system developed in conjunction with Patria, is used by the Air Force Academy in which the system's four simulator units are interconnected, enabling four trainees to fly together in a shared virtual airspace.

The increased use of LVC systems illustrates how the focus of training is now less focussed on traditional flying skills and more on building students' information-processing abilities and achieving better situational awareness.

Left: Finland purchased 28 second-hand Grob 115E/EAs, previously used by the RAF, from UK-based Babcock International in 2016. (Mark Salter)

Below: The student pilot syllabus requires cadets to spend approximately 90 hours on the Grob 115, following elementary and advanced flying courses. (Kevin Wright)

Above: Since their purchase, the Grob 115s have gradually passed through major maintenance checks and a modification programme, including installation of a modern glass cockpit. (Ilmavoimat)

Below left and below right: The 'GO' simulator system developed by Patria for the Grob 115, enables the networking of simulator 'flights' with live aircraft flights to enable students to experience more complex mission scenarios. (Ilmavoimat)

British Aerospace Hawk

On completion of their training on the Grob 115, students join Flying Training Squadron 41, also at Tikkakoski, using its Hawks for their advanced phase training. In December 1977, Finland announced that it would purchase 50 Hawk Mk 51 trainers from British Aerospace. The first Ilmavoimat Hawk (HW-302) arrived from Dunsfold, Surrey, on 16 December 1980, flown by Major Paavo Janhunen. The first four aircraft were built in the UK, with the remaining 46 assembled in Finland and the last (HW-350) delivered in October 1985. In 1990, a batch of seven new Mk 51A aircraft were purchased and delivered direct from the BAE Warton plant, Lancashire, during 1993 and 1994. A third batch of aircraft was obtained in 2007, when 18 second-hand, low-flight-hour Mk 66 aircraft were purchased from Switzerland for 41 million Euro. In 2009, Patria was contracted to upgrade all the Mk 66 airframes.

The Finnish Hawk fleet has been maintained and updated with close cooperation between Finnish Defence Forces Logistics Command and contractor Patria. Work has included life-cycle extension

HW-302 was the first Hawk delivered to the Ilmavoimat from the British Aerospace Dunsfold production line in December 1980. (Ilmavoimat)

Left: Illustrating the three paint schemes used by Finnish AF Hawks, left, the original camouflage, centre, the modern grey scheme and right, the red and white of the former Swiss Hawk Mk66s. (Ilmavoimat/Ville Tuokko)

Below: The former Swiss Mk 66 Hawks have always retained their distinctive appearance in the red and white colour scheme. In late 2022, the Ilmavoimat announced that they would all be repainted in the grey scheme used by the rest of its Hawk fleet. (Kevin Wright)

through fuselage and structural strengthening programmes, and installation of a 'glass cockpit' with modern multifunction displays. Two of these former Swiss aircraft were lost in a collision close to Kauhava, in November 2013. Kauhava AB was closed in 2014 and the Ilmavoimat's Hawk fleet moved to Tikkakoski AB, alongside the Air Force Academy.

By 2020, there were 32 fully modernized Hawks in use with HävLLv 41, which comprised: 16 Mk 66s, seven Mk 51As and nine of the original Mk 51s. More recently, Patria have developed the 'Hawk Link' system to provide a Live, Virtual and Constructive (LVC) training environment for the aircraft and its pilots. The Hawk Link system transmits position information between aircraft utilising radios removed from the Hornets during their mid-life upgrades and new antennas fitted on the Hawk Mk 66s. Contractor Patria developed a Multi-Purpose Controller Unit adapter that communicated between the Hawk mission computers and the repurposed radios. Data can now be transmitted between real aircraft, ground-based aircraft simulators and purely computer-generated elements to enable the construction of complex flight scenarios. This is less expensive than 'live' training and gives trainees many more opportunities to experience large-scale air operations much earlier in their flying careers. The sophistication of the Hawk Link LVC is expected to significantly improve in the near future.

Right: Contractor Patria has upgraded the remaining 16 Hawk Mk 66s and installed 'Hawk Link' equipment to allow them to undertake Live, Virtual and Constructive training in conjunction with flight simulators and computer-generated input. (Mike Butorac)

Below: In 2014, the Ilmavoimat's Hawk fleet moved from Kauhava AB to Tikkakoski to locate alongside the rest of the Air Force Academy. (Mark Salter)

The Hawk is expected to remain in Finnish service until the late 2030s. If so, its career will have spanned six decades and trained pilots from those that went on to fly the Draken and MiG-21 in the 1980s, through all of the Ilmavoimat's F/A-18 Hornet pilots and to those who will soon fly the F-35.

Not only does the Hawk operate in the training role, it has secondary combat roles as an air-defence fighter and light-attack aircraft. Most visible are the aircraft flown by the 'Midnight Hawks', the Finnish Air Force aerobatic team that often carry special markings. They were officially formed in 1997 and have entertained crowds all over Europe with their displays ever since. All team pilots serve as qualified flight instructors at the Air Force Academy.

RADIOACTIVE MONITORING

Above and below: In a potential radiological hazard situation, a Hawk with a specially adapted pylon-mounted device can collect air samples for analysis by Finland's Sätelyturvakeskus (STUK – Radiation Protection Centre). Having flown through an affected area, specialist ground staff in protective gear remove the air filter from the modified tank to measure radiation levels. (Ilmavoimat)

The Midnight Hawks aerobatic team was formed in 1997 and has performed at air shows all over Europe. (Kevin Wright)

Right: Solo Midnight Hawk flyby captured at the 2022 Royal International Air Tattoo (Crown copyright 2022, Cpl Matthews).

Below: In rehearsals for the Finnish Air Force's 100th Anniversary air show in 2018, the Midnight Hawks fly over Jyväskylä, close to the Air Force Academy. (Kevin Wright)

Left: The white smoke used during Midnight Hawks' displays comes from special wing-mounted tanks. (Kevin Wright)

Below: In the lead-up to the August 2021 Aero Baltic Airshow at Gdynia, a joint RAF Red Arrows and Finnish Midnight Hawks formation mount a publicity flyby along the Polish coast. (Mark Salter)

Bottom: A very special paint scheme applied to HW-340 to mark the 40th anniversary of the Hawk in Ilmavoimat service. (Mark Salter)

Chapter 4

Hornet Power

S ince the mid-1990s, Finland's F-18 Hornets have been at the forefront of its air combat capability. The harsh winter conditions in which routine operations are conducted were significant considerations in selecting a replacement for its Saab 35 Drakens and MiG-21s in the early 1990s. The combination of twin-engine safety, rugged, proven design and capable weaponry were major factors in Finland's final decision to purchase 57 F-18C single-seat and seven F-18D two-seat aircraft in 1992. The selection was widely criticised at the time as an 'overly ambitious expansion'. However, it was a wise investment, with the aircraft proving readily adaptable to Finland's evolving defence needs.

The aircraft are fitted with an APG-73 pulse Doppler radar and powered by two General Electric F404-GE-402 turbofans. Armament consists of an M61 Vulcan cannon, a maximum of 12 air-to-air missiles, an ALQ-165 electronics countermeasures system and flare/chaff dispensers. The single-seat aircraft were produced under licence in Finland by the Patria Group with the first F-18C delivered in 1996 and the last in August 2000. The seven two-seat F-18Ds were delivered straight from the US production line, the first four arriving at Pirkkala Air Base on 7 November 1995 direct from the St Louis plant.

The first Ilmavoimat F-18D taxies in at the McDonnell Douglas St Louis plant after its first test flight. (Ilmavoimat)

A large gathering of invited guests and representatives greet the first F-18Ds arriving at Pirkkala Air Base on 7 November 1995 following a direct flight from St Louis. (Ilmavoimat)

Finland's F-18s entered service with three Squadrons. HävLLv 11 was assigned to Lapland Air Command flying from Rovaniemi, with 31 Fighter Squadron (HävLLv 31) at Rissala Air Base, assigned to Karelian Air Command. The third Squadron, HävLLv 21, went to Pirkkala Air Base, Tampere. It was disbanded in June 2014, with most of its aircraft redistributed to HävLLv 11, part of a major reorganisation of the armed forces. The Ilmavoimat still flies its 55 remaining F-18Cs and all seven of its F-18Ds.

After potential F-18 pilots successfully complete their advanced training on the Hawk, they are posted to Rovaniemi or Rissala. Their initial Hornet training usually requires 10–15 hours in the simulator, followed by 4–5 hours in the two-seat F-18Ds, before progressing to the single-seat F-18Cs. Col Tomi Böhm is one of the Ilmavoimat's most experienced F-18 pilots, having accumulated more than 1,500 hours on the type. After completing his flying training on the L-70 Vinka and then the Hawk, he moved to the F-18 in 2000. From 2016 to January 2019, he was the Commanding Officer of HävLLv 31. He explained that:

> The initial operational goal is to train pilots to fly Quick Reaction Alert (QRA) air-policing missions and that takes about a year to achieve. After that, the training becomes more about tactical air warfare as pilots are introduced to the air-to-ground task. To become fully trained in all roles we consider it takes pilots at least five years, but you really never finish learning on such a versatile aircraft.

Above: Seconds before touchdown; a great strength of the F/A-18 Hornet, in Finnish service, has been its ruggedness and ability to operate in Arctic conditions. (Sebastian Viinikainen).

Left: Col Tomi Böhm is one of the Ilmavoimat's most experienced F/A-18 pilots. He has commanded fighter squadron HävLLv 31 and led the Finnish detachment to Red Flag Alaska during October 2018. (Ilmavoimat)

Col Böhm explained how the F-18's capabilities had been transformed during its career. 'For the first 15 years of Ilmavoimat service our F-18s operated solely in the air-to-air role. Between 2006 and 2010 two Mid-Life Update (MLU) programmes transformed it into a true multi-role aircraft.' MLU 1 saw cockpit improvements that included a new APX-111 Identification Friend or Foe transponder and a Tactical Aircraft Moving Map Capability. However, most significant was the introduction of the Joint Helmet Mounted Cueing System for use with the Raytheon AIM-9X Sidewinder. As Col Böhm explained: 'MLU 1 was a big step in F-18 capabilities. It gave us a very capable jet, agile and highly manoeuvrable. The aircraft is very pilot-friendly, easy to fly in air combat. The helmet cueing greatly enhanced our F-18s in air-to-air combat capabilities.'

In February 2008, Northrop Grumman was contracted to deliver 10 'Litening' advanced targeting pod systems for its F-18s, a precursor for the much more ambitious MLU 2 programme that began in 2012. This gave Finnish F-18s a full ground-attack capability, bringing the aircraft up to the F/A-18 standard and improved its inter-connectivity with other air forces. The improvements saw software updates for precision ordnance, replacement of the LCD cockpit displays, a new GPS, installation of the BOL chaff/flare dispenser system and the capability to use improved AIM-120 AMRAAMs. The aircraft's original Finnish Nokia data communication system was replaced with a NATO standard Link 16 compatible system. As Col Böhm explained: 'The new generation of AIM-120 AMRAAMs made the F-18 very good in the beyond-visual-range air fight. That complemented our existing close-in combat capabilities and provides an excellent combination of weapons.' The last MLU 2 aircraft rolled off Patria Aviation's production line on 9 December 2016.

Right: Groundcrew load an AIM-9X on an F-18's wing in Arctic weather. For the first 15 years of its Ilmavoimat career the Hornet performed solely in the air-defence role. (Ilmavoimat)

Below: In February 2008, Finland ordered 10 Litening targeting pods to give its Hornets a precision ground-attack capability. (USAF/A1C Viviam Chiu)

The F-18s first mid-life update programme (MLU 1) greatly improved the F-18s air-to-air capabilities. MLU 2 gave the aircraft a comprehensive avionics refit and a ground attack capability, bringing it up to full F/A-18 standard. (Kevin Wright)

For the first time following integration of the Joint Direct Attack Munition (JDAM) and Joint Stand-Off Weapon (JSOW), completed in December 2017, Finnish F-18s had a precision air-to-ground weapon capability. Col Böhm said: 'We had been training and operating in the air-to-ground role for a few years, but this was a big jump in capability and gave us a lot more flexibility. We now have a strong ground-attack capability to support the Finnish Army and Navy when necessary.'

In April 2016, two F/A-18Cs (HN-410 and HN-419) were ferried to the United States for the preliminary stages of integration work for the Joint Air-to-Surface Standoff (JASSM) missile for the Finnish Hornets. This programme required modification of the aircraft's software and testing the mechanical carriage and the missile's separation on launch. The two aircraft returned to Finland from Patuxent River, Maryland, to Pirkkala Air Base on 9 May 2016. During the ferry flight they were accompanied by an Omega Air Tanker KDC-10. Achievement of full operational

A practice JDAM munition is loaded onto an F/A-18C, part of the capability enhancement delivered by MLU 2. (Ilmavoimat)

Above: Without its own air-refuelling capability, a commercially hired KDC-10 tanker was used to ferry the two F/A-18s to the US for JASSM integration trials. (Ilmavoimat)

Right: A banking HN-466 clearly displays its two JASSM munitions during live launch integration trials in the USA in March 2018. (Ilmavoimat)

capability was marked by two successful JASSM test launches at China lake in early March 2018 from F/A-18D HN-466.

Finland's severe winter weather and near continuous darkness pose major operating difficulties for any air force. Col Böhm explained:

Winter is the most challenging period, but it is not usually any obstacle to us. Even in very snowy and icy conditions we can still manage to taxi and fly. In winter, we often operate in temperatures of -25°C. The jets can manage that, but we place restrictions on the temperatures we operate in, mainly because of pilot considerations. We are concerned about how long pilots could survive, before we could recover them, if they had to eject from their aircraft in the darkness over some isolated forest. We can operate down to limits of -30–35°C. Our long winter means we get a lot more night-flying experience than is possible in more southerly European countries.

Ilmavoimat F/A-18s and their crews have to safely operate through long Arctic winters with sub-zero temperatures. (Ilmavoimat)

An F/A-18 on approach to a winter road-strip landing during Exercise 'Talvinora 21'. (Ilmavoimat/Anne Torvinen)

The Air Force is responsible for the operational level maintenance of its F/A-18s with the Finnish Defence Forces Logistics Command (DFLC) purchasing the material and equipment items required for the Hornet fleet. Patria's role is to perform a significant proportion of regular scheduled aircraft maintenance, repairs and upgrades of the aircraft. Lt Col Harri Korhonen, an engineering officer with the Aircraft Branch of the DFLC, explained that: 'The Air Force performs a small amount of scheduled maintenance to maintain its competencies and capabilities to operate in a crisis situation.' The Air Force asserts that its strategic partnership with a domestic supplier such as Patria, rather than an international company, ensures that its services are available in the event of crisis, when an international partner's support might be withdrawn.'

Patria is responsible for all the major update and maintenance work on the Ilmavoimat's F/A-18 fleet. (Ilmavoimat)

'Frankenhornet'

Finland's Hornets have a very successful operational safety record, with only one major accident. On 8 November 2001, two *Ilmavoimat* F-18Cs collided while on a training flight southeast of Lappajärvi in Western Finland. The pilot of one (HN430) ejected safely. The other (HN413) was seriously injured but successfully made a single engine emergency landing at Pirkkala. It was decided to use part of HN413, combined with part of a severely damaged CF-18B airframe obtained from Canada, to produce another F-18D (HN468). Almost inevitably it became nicknamed by some as the 'Frankenhornet'. It flew on 3 December 2009 after approximately 100,000 hours of rebuilding. Unfortunately, during a test flight on 21 January 2010, it suffered a major control failure that forced the two crew to eject. Both sustained injuries and the aircraft crashed in a forest at Juupajoki, some 200 km/125 miles north of Helsinki.

F-18D HN-468 sometimes described as the 'Frankenhornet,' was assembled from parts of a severely damaged Finnish F-18C and a CF-18B of the Canadian Armed Forces. (Ilmavoimat)

Quick Reaction Alert Operations

Quick Reaction Alert (QRA) missions in support of territorial air-policing operations are a central task for Finland's F/A-18s. The subject is a sensitive one, with officials always reluctant to discuss details of their QRA commitments. Col Böhm explained in 2019:

The main area of Finnish QRA operations is along our southern coast where there is a lot of civilian traffic, plus the major NATO Baltic Air Policing operation. There are frequent missions over the Gulf of Finland, which has become an extremely busy airspace in the last few years. There are lots of QRA missions and pilots are naturally very eager to take part in them to gain operational experience.

Above: At its main operating bases, the F/A-18s can conduct quick reaction alert (QRA) missions from the relative comfort of hardened shelters. (Ilmavoimat)

Left: Like fighter pilots everywhere, Finnish F/A-18 pilots are keen to take part in QRA operations, with the possibility of 'real' intercept missions. (Ilmavoimat)

Launches are controlled and directed by the Finnish Air Operations Centre at Jyväskylä-Tikkakoski Air Base. The number of aircraft on QRA at any one time can be flexible, depending on the threat situation as assessed by the Air Operations Centre. If necessary QRA air-defence missions can be launched by aircraft dispersed across the major operating bases, reserve fields and appropriate civil airfields. The Ilmavoimat asserts that the numbers of aircraft on QRA and their readiness levels 'change to suit the international situation and perceived threat levels'. When launched, F-18s on QRA are guided by controllers from the AOC, usually to intercept aircraft in international airspace. Pilots are tasked to identify the intercepted aircraft type, nationality and tail number. Pilots carry handheld cameras to help with that process too. Any infringements of Finnish airspace are investigated by the Finnish Border Guard service (Rajavartiolaitos) using photographic and radar evidence supplied by the Air Force.

Right: Missions from civil airfields and dispersed road strips often require working in much more austere conditions. (Ilmavoimat)

Below: Live QRA intercept launches are directed by controllers from Finnish and NATO Air Operations Centres. (Stefan Wright-Cole)

This F/A-18C carries an acquisition round AIM-9 on its wing tip. (Kevin Wright)

Baltic Air Policing

Russia's attitude towards NATO enlargement and the nature of many of its air movements to and from Kaliningrad, saw the Alliance establish its 'Baltic Air Policing mission' at Šiauliai Air Base in Lithuania, following the accession of the three Baltic states to NATO in 2004. Continuously since then, NATO member states have operated fighter aircraft from there on a rotational basis. Naturally Finland's long land border with the Russian Federation and its close proximity across the Gulf of Finland, give it a strong interest in aircraft movements approaching all its borders.

Following Russia's occupation of Crimea in 2014, NATO's Baltic Air Policing mission expanded with the introduction of a second operating base at Ämari in Estonia, part of the Alliance's wider 'Enhanced Air Policing' initiative. These air defence operations are managed from the Combined Air Operations Centre (CAOC) at Udem, Germany. Command of the CAOC rotates between Germany and Belgium and is staffed by more than 180 personnel from 18 NATO nations.

Finland's response in the last 20 years has seen the gradual strengthening of its air-defence network through unilateral efforts and closer cooperation with both its Nordic neighbours and NATO. While Finland has maintained responsibility for its own territorial air defence, its effectiveness has been enhanced by greater cooperation with the NATO mission and, in particular, the Alliance's network of air defence radars and operations centres. Especially important in this context is the Baltic Air Surveillance Network (BALTNET) at Karmėlava, Lithuania and the associated NATO Air Operations Control Centre in each Baltic state. For interceptions of Russian Federation and other unidentified aircraft over the Gulf of Finland, it is not unusual to have a pair of NATO fighters shadowing Russian aircraft in the southern part of the Gulf, with Finnish F-18s covering the northern area.

The air-policing mission created very specific training needs among all the contributing NATO countries, and is met by a regular series of short 'Ramstein Alloy' exercises. Held since 2016, and

Above: Directed by NATO and Finnish authorities, interceptions of Russian aircraft have become routine events in recent years. This Russian SU-27 t was flying over the Gulf of Finland in January 2022. (Ilmavoimat)

Right: Since 2016, regular NATO 'Ramstein Alloy' exercises have provided Finnish pilots with opportunities to practice multiple interception and emergency scenarios. (Ilmavoimat)

hosted by the Baltic states and with three iterations in 2022, both Finnish and Swedish aircraft routinely take part in them. Exercise scenarios include intercepts of slow-moving aircraft and escorting simulated civilian airliners that have suffered communication loss. Other training includes dealing with a simulated crew ejection situation, activation of the search and rescue chain, aerial refuelling and dissimilar air combat training.

Aerial Refuelling

A significant constraint on the Finnish Air Force's Hornets capabilities has been the lack of an indigenous air-refuelling capability. That shortfall has been addressed for some years by working with tanker equipped NATO air forces, especially the United States.

One early exercise involved the British. RAF Group Captain Tony Gumby was the Commanding Officer of 10 Squadron, then flying VC-10 tanker-transport aircraft. He explained that: 'In August 2001, we flew a single VC-10 to Rovaniemi and refuelled our 20(R) Squadron Harriers along the way for exercise 'Lone Kestrel'. We spent four or five days there and flew local air-refuelling sorties to qualify the Finns in in-flight refuelling. As they did not have any tanker capability of their own, it was quite a big thing.'

Above: US Air Force KC-135R tanker aircraft, often from the 100th Air Refuelling Wing (ARW) at RAF Mildenhall, have regularly provided air-refuelling training and exercise support for Ilmavoimat F/A-18s. (Ilmavoimat)

Left: In 2001, RAF VC-10 tankers provided the Ilmavoimat with some of its early opportunities to practise aerial refuelling. (Ilmavoimat)

Below: Cross-national training with the Swedish Air Force can provide opportunities for aerial-refuelling practice with Flygvapnet C-130s. (Ilmavoimat)

Subsequently such training has traditionally been undertaken within the context of NATO's 'Partnership For Peace' exercises that include non-member states. Since 2009 the USAFE's (US Air Forces in Europe) 100th Air Refuelling Wing KC-135Rs from RAF Mildenhall, Suffolk, have regularly deployed to Finland to conduct aerial-refuelling training with Finnish Air Force Hornets. These efforts have sometimes been augmented by USAF Air National Guard tanker units and on occasion US Marine Corps KC-130Js.

Red Flag-Alaska

The most ambitious of overseas deployments so far was the Ilmavoimat's participation in exercise Red Flag Alaska 19-1, from 4 to 19 October 2018, at Eielson AFB, Alaska. Col Böhm was the operational commander for this first Finnish participation in a Red Flag exercise. Preparations were begun about 18 months previously for the deployment of six F-18s and around 70 personnel. As he explained, 'The most challenging part was the logistics. We were not so concerned by Alaska's environment; we expected it to be similar to Finland. So, it was a bit of a surprise when the weather was warm and sunny. We arrived in Alaska two weeks prior to Red Flag, taking part first in Exercise Distant Frontier One where we worked with American units, mainly on air-to-air missions.' In the two weeks following Red Flag, the Finns concentrated on air-to-ground operations in Distant Frontier Two. He continued:

Our flying operations were fully supported by the USAF tanker fleet. When we deployed to Alaska we left Finland, flew close to Iceland, through to Bangor Air National Guard Base in Maine. The aircraft stopped there for two nights before completing the second leg to Alaska. For some years we have had tanker training, usually twice a year and so our F-18 pilots are qualified for air-to-air refuelling. However, the 9.5-hour flight with 10 refuellings was new to us; it created an extra pressure for the pilots but was completed safely and with no problems.

The Red Flag exercise was very good, a complex environment with a lot of electronic warfare assets, a lot of aircraft in the same airspace, flying combined operations with American and South Korean aircraft and ground units. It went well. It was complicated, challenging, very educational and from my perspective we did a very good job. We were able to fight together at an equal level with the Americans. I was very pleased with the performance of our pilots, technicians and everyone that took part.

The continual modernisation of F/A-18s, the addition of new weapon capabilities and its ability to air-refuel, albeit in conjunction with its allies, together with rigorous training all demonstrate that Finland possesses a modern, capable and efficient air force. Its next step will take it to the forefront of modern military aviation.

Eielson AFB hosted the Ilmavoimat's first participation in 'Red Flag Alaska' during October 2018 when F/A-18s deployed there. (Ilmavoimat)

Above: Exercise 'Distant Thunder' provided opportunities to train with USAF Alaskan-based F-22A Raptors. (Ilmavoimat)

Left: Despite being in service for nearly 30 years Finland's F/A-18s remain agile and formidable opponents to any potential aggressors. (Mark Salter)

Below: Specially marked HN-421 is piloted by Capt Aleksi Ritvos, the Finnish F/A-18 solo display pilot, at Ostrava Airport in September 2022. (Ilmavoimat)

Chapter 5
From 'HX' to F-35

The F/A-18 Hornet has served Finland extremely well. However, its advancing age means replacement is necessary with a 2030 out-of-service date envisaged for it. The HX (Hornet replacement) fighter programme was launched in 2015 to begin its replacement. It is the most expensive procurement programme the Finnish Defence Forces have engaged in to date. The HX programme is intended to replace the F-18s on a one-for-one basis and they are expected to remain in service until the 2060s. Specifications require that the replacement aircraft is capable of performing air defence, ground and maritime attack tasks.

In April 2018, the Finnish Defence Forces sent a Request for Quotation (RFQ) to the French, British, Swedish and US governments. These sought detailed submissions from Boeing for its F/A-18 Super Hornet, from Dassault for the Rafale, from BAE for the Eurofighter Typhoon, from Lockheed Martin for the F-35A and from Saab for its Gripen E/F. By January 2019, all five companies had responded. Another major requirement was that the winning manufacturer would provide significant work for Finnish companies in the production phase and the subsequent support contracts.

The 100th anniversary of The *Ilmavoimat*'s formation was marked in 2018. A public airshow at Tikkakoski marked the centenary of the Finnish Air Force with aircraft from four of the five HX competitors on display. This gave the Ilmavoimat, and the Finnish public, an opportunity to see most of the HX contenders close together. The French Air Force sent Rafales, Sweden the Gripen E/F models, the US a pair of EA-18G Growlers, and Eurofighter was represented by Typhoon contingents from Italy, Germany, Spain and the UK. Away from the public gaze, the five contenders were asked to assemble bids for the project and explain how their platforms met Finnish specifications.

The promise to replace the existing Hornet fleet on a one-for-one basis, came under some pressure due to the huge cost of the HX programme. Maj Gen Lauri Puranen, the HX Programme Director at the Finnish Ministry of Defence, said this was necessary to maintain a credible capability to defend the country.

Defending Finland's airspace and supporting the other services engaged in combat requires that a sufficient number of fighters are available in all situations… The operational range of a fighter is about 500 km, which means that in Finland it is necessary to be able to operate simultaneously in two directions at once. In one operational direction, several four-fighter sections are needed, and when necessary, they will have to be fuelled and

This page and opposite page: In June 2018 the Finnish Air Force marked the 100th anniversary of the Ilmavoimat's formation with a public air show at Tikkakoski. It enabled the Finnish public to see the HX contenders. Sweden sent a Saab Gripen (*left*), Boeing a specialist electronic warfare EA-18G 'Growler' (*below*). The French contender Dassault was represented by a pair of Rafales (*bottom*). Eurofighter sent examples from the Italian Air Force (*opposite above*), Spain, (*opposite below*) Germany and the UK. (All photos Stefan Wright-Cole).

As part of its HX bid, a Lockheed Martin pilot demonstrates the F-35 simulator to Finnish pilots. (Lockheed Martin).

armed on the ground. Some of the fleet are always out of use because of servicing. Undisputedly the new fighters will be more effective than the Hornet fleet, but … the arming and fuelling time required on the ground for a new sortie needs to be roughly the same. In view of the Defence Forces' tasks, the full replacement of the Hornet fleet requires that the current number of [64] fighters will be kept.

A more specific RFQ (request for quote) was issued in the second half of 2019 and was followed by a second phase of negotiations with the competing companies.

HX Challenge Event

The Ilmavoimat organised an 'HX Challenge' to test the capabilities of the candidate aircraft, centred on Tampere-Pirkkala Air Base, from 9 January to 26 February 2020. The event was regarded as particularly important because the successful aircraft had to be able to perform well in the harshest of Finnish winter conditions. While it was expected that these modern multi-role fighters could manage low temperatures and freezing cold, once temperatures fall to around 0°C, the combination of rain, freezing drizzle, sleet and snow can adversely affect the performance of electro-optical and other sensor equipment. Evaluations of the different candidate's operational turnaround and rearming times were also a high priority because of the implications for the overall mission tempo during wartime operations.

Each aircraft type was to complete the assigned tasks over a scheduled week-long period. For the Eurofighter Typhoon that was 9–17 January 2020 and involved two aircraft loaned from the RAF's 41 Squadron. Dassault's Rafales were present from 20 to 28 January 2020 and Saab followed with two Gripen NG's from 29 January to 6 February. The Gripens were demonstrated to be offered in conjunction with Sweden's 'Global Eye' platform based on the Bombardier Global 6000/6500 aircraft. The two F-35As from 7 to 17 February 2020 belonged to the 308 Fighter Squadron at Luke AFBs, USA. Billie Flynn, one of the Lockheed civilian F-35 test pilots, who brought one of the aircraft to Finland, faced a 10-hour flight with 11 aerial refuellings from Finland to Dover AFB, USA, on his return trip. The Super Hornet element (from 18 to 26 February) comprised an F/A-18E, an F/A-18F and an

The Typhoon was the first contender to be evaluated by the Finns in mid-January 2020 when two RAF aircraft visited Pirkkala AB. (Ilmavoimat)

Saab deployed two Gripen NGs to Finland for the challenge event. As part of its bid for the HX contract it offered an AEW capability with modified Bombardier Global 6000/6500 platforms. (Ilmavoimat)

Lockheed Martin's offering saw two F-35As sent to Finland requiring a 10-hour non-stop flight from Dover AFB, USA, with multiple air refuellings. (Ilmavoimat)

EA-18G Growler. Boeing's offer was later revised to be a mix of 50 F/A-18 E and Fs and 14 specialist electronic warfare EA-18Gs. Alongside the flying element of the event there were significant simulator and ground-based activities to verify the data already provided by the competitors in their written bids.

A second phase of negotiations followed during 2020 with the contenders submitting their final tender documents by 30 April 2021. On 10 December 2021, the Finnish government announced its decision to opt for the F-35A Lightning II at an estimated programme cost of 10 billion Euro. One significant factor said to have contributed to the F-35s selection was that it was at a much earlier stage in its development life. Therefore, it was more likely to be suitable for further major enhancements during its service career compared to its competitors.

Initial plans envisage the first Hornets being phased out from 2025 with their complete replacement scheduled between 2028 and 2030. In 2025, the first Finnish F-35As will enter service to train Ilmavoimat personnel in the United States, and delivery of the first airframes to Finland are expected in 2026, to be completed by 2030. The procurement contracts are for 64 multi-role Block 4 configuration F-35As plus 'aircraft engines and maintenance equipment, systems, spare parts, replacement equipment, training equipment and servicing needed for use and maintenance. The agreement includes F-35-type training for Finnish flying and technical personnel. Finnish industrial participation was a significant element of the HX programme and was expected to be at 30 percent of the total contract price. The most significant elements of that industrial participation includes production of F-35 front fuselages in Finland, plus some 'structural components and an equipment testing and maintenance capability'. Finland was also offered final assembly of the P &W engines for Ilmavoimat aircraft. While many precise details remain to be agreed, the weapon systems identified so far for the Finnish fleet include: AMRAAMs, Sidewinders, SDB I and II, JDAM-family weaponry, JSM and JASSM-ER. Additional weapon fits will evolve as new systems become operational. In May 2022, Air Force Commander Brigadier General Juha-Pekka Keränen announced that the first of Finland's F-35s will be assigned to Lapland Air Command at Rovaniemi from 2026.

The AIM-120 advanced medium-range air-to-air missile (AMRAAM) is used by the F/A-18s and in the near future the F-35As. (Ilmavoimat)

Chapter 6

Transport and Intelligence

The Ilmavoimat's air-support capability is a modest one, managed through Satakunta Air Command and the Air Support Squadron centred on its Headquarters at Tampere-Pirkkala Air Base. Finland's heavy and strategic airlift needs are met through membership of NATO's Strategic Airlift Capability programme. The programme operates three jointly owned C-17 transports operated by the Heavy Airlift Wing at Papa AB in Hungary. Finland's manpower contribution is four staff. Its share gives Finland 100-flight hours per year.

The Air Support Squadron's flying element comprises an HQ and four Operational Flights. One Flight operates two of Finland's C-295M aircraft in the transport role, Two Flight has three LJ35As, Three Flight uses the third Finnish C-295M configured in the SIGINT role, and Four Flight six PC-12NGs.

Prior to the delivery of its first two C-295Ms in 2007, and a third in 2011, the Ilmavoimat operated three Fokker F-27s in similar transport roles since 1980. Most C-295M missions are flown to support routine Air Force and Army operations, but the aircraft can be configured for para-dropping and MEDEVAC missions. The aircraft have been used to support Finnish contingents taking part in UN and international operations including those in Chad, Afghanistan and Kosovo. The C-295s have long built a reputation for versatility and reliability, capable of rough field and road-strip operations.

Finland's heavy airlift needs are met through its participation in NATO's Strategic Airlift Capability programme that uses three C-17 Globemasters. (Gerard van der Schaaf)

Satakunta Air Command is responsible for the Ilmavoimat's transport assets at Tampere-Pirkkala AB, including its long-serving and very versatile Learjet LJ35As. (Kevin Wright)

Finland received two transport C295Ms in 2007; CC-3 is seen here turning on final approach to Tampere airfield. (Sebastian Viinikainen)

Right: A load master prepares a C295M's side cargo door for a paratroop jump. (Ilmavoimat)

Below: Taxiing in at Pori airport in Finland, C295Ms have been used to support Finnish troop deployments in Europe, Africa, the Middle East and Afghanistan. (Sebastian Viinikainen)

The most secretive element of Ilmavoimat operations is its airborne SIGINT (signal intelligence) capability. The standard transport Fokker F27 FF-2 was withdrawn in 2004 followed by the FF-3 in 2013. The SIGINT F-27 platform, FF-1, only converted to the role in 1996, remained in service until 2015. In 2010, a replacement system was ordered from Lockheed in the form of its 'Dragon Shield' SIGINT equipment described as a 'containerised roll-on-roll-off surveillance system' to be supplied together with associated ground stations and communications terminals. Like most similar modern systems, its open architecture design will allow it to be more easily upgraded and reconfigured to support evolving mission needs. The airframe selected for modification, CC-1, was delivered in March 2007 and served for the first few years as a standard transport aircraft. The aircraft modification, purchase and installation of the Dragon Shield system was originally priced at 112M Euro. Delivered back to the Ilmavoimat in 2013, the Dragon Shield 'control system' experienced significant integration issues and it was not until 2017 that some of the final components became available, resulting in a compensation payment from Lockheed. The Finnish Air Force announced full operational capability of the system on 12 February 2018.

Finland operates three Learjet 35ASs, which were purchased in 1982 to replace its obsolete Soviet Il-28s bombers, used for target-towing missions and some maritime patrol operations. Fitted with external hardpoints, they have proved versatile across a wide variety of tasks. Roles have included use as VIP transport, maritime patrol, target-towing, photo-reconnaissance, fallout monitoring, aerial photographic, search and rescue, air sampling, electronic-warfare and SIGINT platforms. A 2018 service-life extension programme saw a significant modification programme including the updating of the avionics fit, a changed passenger compartment seating arrangement and improved photographic capabilities.

F-27 FF-1 was converted to the SIGINT role in 1996 and only retired in 2015. The large under-fuselage aerial array betrays its SIGINT role. (Sebastian Viinikainen)

C295M CC-1 was converted to the SIGINT role and delivered to the Ilmavoimat in 2013, but completion of its 'Dragon Shield' equipment fit was not fully completed until early 2018. (Sebastian Viinikainen)

Three Learjets were purchased in 1982 and operated in a wide variety of roles including target towing, survey photography, CASEVAC and VIP transport to name just some. (Kevin Wright)

Fitted with an underwing RM-30B 'Reeling machine-launcher' used for target towing in 2016, Finnish Learjets long used this green-brown camouflage scheme. (Sebastian Viinikainen)

Finnish Learjets regularly take part in the annual road-strip exercises such as 'Baana 20' that used the Hosio road strip, flying training and liaison missions. (Ilmavoimat)

A 2018 service-life extension programme updated the cockpit and the aircraft's avionics and modified the passenger compartment layout. (Mark Salter)

For many years six Piper PA-31-350 Navajo Chieftans were operated by the Ilmavoimat for general transport duties. (Sami Niemeläinen)

Ten Valmet-produced L-90 Redigo aircraft were used from 1992 to 2013 in liaison roles. (Sami Niemeläinen)

In 2009, the Finnish Air Force selected the Pilatus PC-12NG to replace its aging Piper Chieftains and domestically-produced Valmet Redigos, in the passenger and light cargo communications role. The first was delivered on 1 July 2010 with initial crew training undertaken by the manufacturer. The six aircraft have since proved well suited to their role and regularly demonstrate their capability to operate from dispersed sites and highway runways. On 19 March 2020, the PC-12NG fleet passed 30,000 flight hours.

Sitting outside the Pilatus plant in Switzerland, the PC-12NG was selected to replace the Ilmavoimat's Piper Chieftans and Valmet Redigos in 2009. (Ilmavoimat)

Disassembled for major manufacturer maintenance, in 2020 Finland's PC-12NG fleet passed the 30,000-flight-hour mark. (Ilmavoimat)

The first of the six-aircraft PC-12NG fleet was delivered in July 2010 and has proved extremely versatile. (Kevin Wright)

Although a comparatively large single-engined aircraft, the PC-12NG has good short-field performance that makes it ideal for keeping dispersed sites supplied. (Kevin Wright)

Above and below: The PC-12NG's cabin interior can be readily reconfigured for passenger or transport operations. It can also be set up for casualty evacuation tasks. (Ilmavoimat)

Chapter 7

Wartime and Dispersed Operations

While the peacetime strength of the Ilmavoimat is just over 2,000 members, it expands massively to around 38,000 on full mobilisation. The limited number of Ilmavoimat main operating bases, even when supplemented by the substantial number of civil airfields available, has meant dispersed operations have long been a major feature of Finland's air-war planning and preparations.

When ordered, aircraft and ground support units disperse from their main operating bases to civilian airfields and road strips on the expectation that the three main bases would be pre-targeted by guided missiles and so would quickly become unusable. Aircraft would move to the pre-selected locations where they would be joined by what has been described as 'an air-field's worth of truck-mounted infrastructure' comprising all the major support services and force protection elements. The dispersal arrangements involve moving to new locations and once there, always moving aircraft between the different road bases and fixed airfield locations. Doing this reduces vulnerability by making it much more difficult for the enemy to catch aircraft on the ground. At each location, groundcrews are ready to refuel and rearm aircraft sent to them by battle-space controllers.

An F/A-18 just before touchdown on the Hosio road strip during exercise Baana 20. Dispersed operations are an integral part of Ilmavoimat's war planning. (Ilmavoimat /Anne Torvinen)

For road-strip operations, all the essential airfield services have to be available including air traffic control. (Ilmavoimat)

The procedure has been described as being similar to a Formula-1 pit stop. During Exercise Ruska 17, Lt Col Ville Hakala of Air Force Command explained that: 'There are no clear advantages in using a road base as opposed to a civilian airfield. The usability and benefits of a base largely depend on the ground support units available there.' For the aircrews, 'There are no major challenges when operating from an unfamiliar airfield; our pilots are constantly practising operations from different airports.'

As an example of dispersed operations, a pair of F/A-18s landing at the Vierema road strip during Exercise Ruska 17 taxied to the rearm point at the end of the runway. A combined team of regulars,

Smaller civilian airfields, such as this one at Ylivieska, are an essential part of Finland's dispersed operations' doctrine. (Ilmavoimat)

Above and below: At the Virttaa road strip, a groundcrew member attaches fins to an AIM-9 'Sidewinder' on an F/A-18, while others begin manhandling an AMRAAM into position during Exercise Baana 21. These exercises provide valuable training for conscripts and reservists. (Ilmavoimat)

reservists and conscripts rapidly got to work. A fuel tanker moved in close, and as an engine was running, 'hot refuelling' was required. Air-to-air missiles were manhandled into position and secured in place on each of the aircraft's empty wing hard points. Heavily armed force protection troops are close by, securing the site just in case of attack by enemy special forces. While the groundcrews are working around the aircraft, the pilots are being cockpit briefed for their next mission by controllers. Once refuelled, rearmed and re-briefed the two Hornets are ready to go again. They might be held on the ground, engines running, at the highway strip until required, or launched immediately from the highway strip straight back into the air battle.

Ever since the first road strip (Lentokoneiden varalaskupaikka) was built in 1965, Finland has retained an officially undisclosed number of such emergency highway strips for wartime use. Of the more than 20 that are known, some are adjacent to existing airfields available for use if the main runway becomes unusable. However, the majority are in comparatively remote locations, away from significant population centres. Individual layouts vary, but each strip usually consists of a widened section of roadway 1,500–3,000m long. All have turning and parking areas at each end, some being much more extensive than others. A significant number have groundworks installed for mobile arrestor gear equipment to be set up for fast jet operations.

While the few European countries that used highway strips largely abandoned their use after the end of the Cold War, the Finnish Defence Forces continued to regularly practise operations from them for a few days each year. In recent years, working in rotation, each of Finland's Air Commands have sponsored an annual exercise known as 'Baana' in which a road strip is temporarily activated. This requires closure of the road to public use for several days and often a small exclusion zone created around it for support operations and related military training to take place. As well as the aircraft,

While aircraft are refuelled and rearmed, pilots are radio-briefed for their next mission by controllers at an Air Operations Centre. (Ilmavoimat)

other support systems are brought in including handling equipment and support personnel (including force protection troops, servicing, refuelling and aircraft armament personnel) together with mobile command and control elements. Such exercises can involve around 400 personnel and involve all categories of conscripts and reservists. In 2015, Swedish AF Gripens participated in the road-strip exercise for the first time and have regularly done so ever since.

Pre-exercise preparation for pilots usually involves staff undertaking a detailed study of the location and successfully flying simulated day and night sorties from the road base. Their first real day and night road-strip sorties are flown with an instructor pilot. The second sortie is a solo one. Flying these sorties poses unusual challenges as the strips are generally much narrower than standard airfields where engine or brake failure can be particularly serious. Many road strips are edged with trees, which pose visibility and additional turbulence issues.

Above: A Swedish Gripen takes off from the Hosio road strip during Baana 15. Since their first participation in 2015, Swedish Gripens have regularly taken part in these exercises. (Louise Levin/ Swedish Armed Forces)

Left: An F/A-18D taxies for departure from the Virttaa road strip. Pilots new to these operations make their first landing and take-off with an experienced instructor pilot in a two-seat aircraft. (Ilmavoimat)

The length of the highway strips is adequate for most operations. Some strips may have mobile cable arresting gear equipment installed to enable the F-18s to practise tailhook landings for use in wet weather or iced-covered road situations. The arrestor cable systems are more tightly rigged than at standard airfields and can stop the aircraft within 150m, a much shorter distance than when used at most main operating bases. At some strips, operations are restricted to daylight flying because of the concerns of local farmers. Where the strips are not adequately fenced, they tend to be used only for daylight operations because of the possibility that large wild animals may wander onto the runway at night.

For night or poor weather operations, a Tactical Instrument Landing System is used to provide a precision approach capability with the addition of mobile runway lights and sometimes a Precision Approach Path Indicator. However, once the aircraft is on the ground and taxies off the runway it can be in complete darkness. Night-vision goggles are used by crews in these situations where there is limited

Sparks fly as an F/A-18C touches down on the Lusi road strip during Baana 19. Many of these sites can accommodate mobile arrestor gear for fast-jet operations. (Ilmavoimat)

Taking the wire at Lusi. At road strips, the arrestor gear cables are more tightly rigged and can stop an aircraft within 150 metres. (Ilmavoimat)

After each arrested landing, crews reset the wire for the next aircraft to land. (Ilmavoimat)

An F/A-18 climbs away from a road strip. Many of these locations are surrounded by high wire fences to prevent large wild animals wandering onto the 'runways', especially during night operations. (Ilmavoimat /AnneTorvinen)

or no lighting available. As well as combat-capable aircraft being dispersed, so too are the Air Force's transport and flight-training assets, the latter dividing into a number of support flights for liaison and light transport tasks. Although it is these dramatic operations from road strips by the F-18s that attract the most public attention, other types also take advantages of the opportunity to practise their skills. During 'Baana' exercises, aircraft generally operate from their home bases. Some perform touch-and-go approaches, with others making full-stop landings and then 'hot refuelling' at the road strip. Total movements can exceed more than 200 per day as new pilots qualify and experienced ones requalify.

Landing on the Jokioinen road strip during Baana 18, the PC-12NG, with good field performance, has proved its value in support of these operations. (Ilmavoimat)

As well as training combat aircraft pilots, road strip operations are also useful training opportunities for the C295M transport crews in narrow runway operations. (Ilmavoimat)

Hawks are regular participants in road-strip exercises, such as this one lifting off from Hosio during Baana 20. (Ilmavoimat /Anne Torvinen)

FINNISH ROAD STRIPS

Alavus Highway Strip

Location: On road 66, about 8km/5 miles northwest of Alavus.
Runways: 17/35, 2600m/8,500ft
Features: Parking loops at northern and southern ends.

Jokioinen Highway Strip

Location: On National route 2, about 5km/3 miles northeast of Jokioinen.
Runways: 14/32, 2100m/7,000ft
Features: Parking loops at both ends, prepared for a portable arrestor cable installation. Used for Exercise Baana 18.

Helsinki Vantaa Highway Strip

Location: To the northwestern side of the Helsinki Vantaa airport, on the road to Katriinantie / Katrinevägen. Currently believed to be unused.
Runways: 02/20, 1500m/5,000ft
Features: Taxiways, apron on the southwest end, which was a taxiway to Vantaa airport.

Hosio Highway Strip

Location: Part of route 924, approximately 6km/4 miles southwest of Hosio, Lapland.
Runways: 06/24, 2000m/6,500ft
Features: A parking loop is located at each end of the runway, with a prepared installation for a mobile arrestor cable. Used for Exercises Baana 15 and 20.

During the Ruska-20 series of exercises, an F/A-18C sits between the trees at the Hosio road strip with wings folded, being checked over by groundcrew. (Ilmavoimat)

Järvitalo Highway Strip

Location: On road 822, about 10km/6 miles southeast of Kärsämä.
Runways: 12/30, 2500m/8,000ft

Joutsa Highway Strip

Location: On highway 4 on the northern limits of Joutsa.
Runways: 17/35, 2500m/8,000ft

Used for Exercise Baana 22

During Baana 22 the Joutsa road strip was made operational from 25 to 30 September 2022. For road-strip operations, force protection is a major consideration with aircraft and areas around the road strips heavily guarded. (*above*) A groundcrew member attaches fins to an AMRAAM on the underwing pylon of an F/A-18. (*right*) In combat kit, another crew member refuels a Hornet. (*overleaf top*) Refuelling from a road tanker continues in the gathering darkness as another F/A-18 is prepared for a night sortie. Most road strips are capable of supporting round the clock operations. (*overleaf bottom*) (All images Ilmavoimat)

Kankanpää Highway Strip
Location: On National Road 23, about 8km/5 miles northwest of Kankanpää.
Runways: 12/30, 2600m/8,500ft

Kauhava Highway Strip
Location: On road 63 about 3km/2 miles northeast of Kauhava airfield.
Runways: 04/22, 1500m//5,000ft
Features: There is a hard stand site at each end, in the southwest and northeast. Prepared installation for an arrestor cable.

Lusi Highway Strip
Location: On National Road 5, about 12km/7.5 miles northeast of Heinola.
Runways: 06/24, 2500m/8,200ft
Features: QRA loop at the northeastern end. Prepared installation for an arrestor cable. Used for Baana 2016 and 2019 exercises.

A 2018 satellite image shows the parking loops at each end of the Lusi highway strip. At the northern end (left-hand side) there is larger area for ground equipment and space to work on the parked aircraft. (Google Earth)

Mikkeli Highway Strip
Location: On road 72, about 8km/5 miles northeast of Mikkeli.
Runways: 17/35, 2500m/8,200ft

Niinisalo Highway Strip
Location: Located on road 23, about 1km/half mile north of Niinsalo.
Runways: 05/23, 3500m/11,500ft

Pirkkala Highway Strip
Location: On road 3003, about 10km/6 miles southwest of Tampere, immediately next to Tampere-Pirkkala airfield, accessible via short taxiway to HAS area.

Runways: 18/36, 1500m/5,000ft
Features: Taxiway to the airfield.

Pudasjärvi Highway Strip
Location: On National Road 78, about 6km/4 miles northwest of Pudasjärvi, immediately west of the airfield accessible via taxiway from main airfield.
Runways: 14/32, 1500m/5,000ft

Rotimojoki Highway Strip
Location: On National Road 88, about 8km/5 miles northwest of Salahmi.
Runways: 14/32, 3000m/10,000ft
Features: There are two parking loops, one 600m/2,000ft away from the southern end and one 1500m/5,000ft from the northern end.

Rovaniemi Highway Strip
Location: R9523 west of the airport. Sometimes referred to as Norvatie. Readiness areas in the north and south. Connection to the airfield available. The runway is located immediately west of Rovaniemi Air Base. Used during Exercise Talvinorva 21.
Runways: 01/19, 1600m/5,200ft
Features: Taxiway to the airfield.

Exercise Talvinorva 21
While standard weather conditions can make off-airfield operations challenging, Finland's severe winter weather and near constant darkness can add a whole new level of difficulty. On 24–25 February 2021 Exercise 'Talvinorva 21' took place on a road strip just outside the perimeter of Rovaniemi Airport, also the headquarters of Lapland Air Command. It tested the Air Force's ability to rapidly set up and operate its F/A-18s from selected road strips in Finland's Arctic winter.

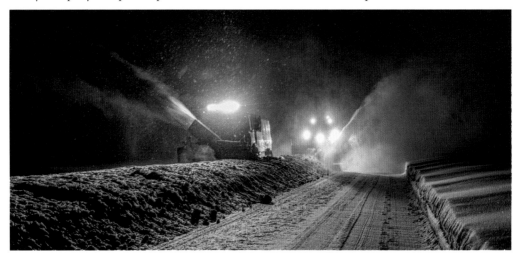

(Ilmavoimat /Anne Torvinen)

On the evening before the exercise, the road adjacent to the airfield was closed and the airport's operational staff from Finavia worked overnight to clear a large depth of snow from the road strip and then melt ice off the road surface. Once the surface was clear, temporary runway lighting was put in place, and communications and air traffic control equipment installed. Following a dawn inspection of the runway, flight operations began and Lapland Air Command accomplished its goal of launching three waves of aircraft, despite heavy snowfall throughout the afternoon.

Above and below: (Ilmavoimat /Anne Torvinen)

Above and below: (Ilmavoimat /Anne Torvinen)

Tervo Highway Strip
Location: On road 551, about 2km/6,500ft southeast of Tervo.
Runways: 13/31, 3000m/10,000ft

Varkhaus Highway Strip
Location: About 10km/6 miles south of Varkhaus.
Runways: 03/21, 2300m/7,500ft

Vierema Highway Strip (Lentokoneiden varalaskupaikka)
Location: On route 88, 2km/1.25 miles northwest of Vierema
Runways: 34/16, 1500m/5,000ft
Features: Parking areas at each end, used for Exercise Baana 17.

A few seconds from touchdown on the Vierema road strip during Exercise Baana 17. (Ilmavoimat/Joni Malkamäki)

Virttaa Highway Strip

Location: On National Road 41 about 2km/1.25 miles north-northeast of Virttaa.

Runways: 18/36, 3000m/10,000ft

Features: Parking loop at each side. In the south prepared installation for an arrestor cable. Used for Exercise Baana 21.

Exercise Baana 21 saw activation of the Virttaa road strip. With more limited parking space available than usual, the F/A-18's are parked among trees at each end of the runway. (Ilmavoimat)

When parked among trees, the F/A-18s folding wings, originally designed for its use on US Navy aircraft carriers, can help create the extra space required. (Ilmavoimat)

When aircraft use the arrestor gear at road strips, it is essential that they do so absolutely on the runway centreline as these are much narrower than those at most airfields. Missing the precise centreline, even minimally, can mean that the aircraft can easily veer towards the soft ground and often trees close to the runway edge. (Ilmavoimat)

Vuojärvi Highway Strip
Location: Approximately 3km/10,000ft southwest of Vuojärvi.
Runways: 05/23, 2500m/8,200ft
Installations: There are QRA areas at each end.

Ylläksentie Highway Strip
Location: On road 80 about14km/9 miles west-southwest of Kittilä.
Runways: 01/19, 2500m/8,200ft
Installations: A hard stand area at each end.

Chapter 8

Finnish Army and Border Control Aircraft

Responsibility for its aviation element was passed to the Army from the Air Force at the end of the 1990s. The Finnish Army (Maavoimat) operates 20 NH-90 and seven MD500 helicopters as part of the Utti Jaeger Regiment's Helicopter Battalion (HELIBN) based at Utti airfield near Kouvola. Student rotary wing pilots start on their 'HH1' helicopter training flying the MD500s, including an element of night flying, while still undergraduates at the National Defence University. Once pilots graduate, they are promoted to Lieutenant and move onto their HH2 flight-training programme. A significant part of this involves learning to effectively use night-vision goggles (NVG) on the MD500s. The course involves basic night-flying techniques and navigation, emergency handling and landing procedures in terrain as well as navigation with NVGs.

The NH-90s were ordered in 2001, gradually entering service from 2008 to 2015, and with Soviet-era Mi-8s retired in 2010. The first was assembled in France with the remainder by Patria. The helicopters work in support of all the Finnish armed services in a wide range of roles. For the army this mainly

Student helicopter pilots commence training on the MD500 helicopter, which first entered Finnish service in 1975. (Sebastian Viinikainen)

In autumn 2022, the first MD500E appeared in a new all-over-black paint scheme. (Sebastian Viinikainen)

From 2008, 20 NH-90s gradually entered Finnish service as replacements for old Soviet Mi-8s. (Crown Copyright/ Cpl Laurence RAF)

Flares are essential for operations in areas where SAMs (surface-to-air missiles) or MANPADS (man-portable air defence systems) pose a significant threat. (Stefan Wright-Cole)

involves tactical support tasks and working with Finnish special forces of the Special Jaeger Battalion. For the Finnish Navy (Merivoimat), this can involve transport and tactical mine-laying operations alongside combat search and rescue tasks for the Air Force. It also works in support of the Border Guard and in conjunction with the police and civil authorities for MEDEVAC tasks and general search and rescue duties. The NH-90s have been used in support of operations in Afghanistan and Kosovo.

Patria is contracted to provide maintenance and support to the Finnish Army NH-90 force in a custom-designed hangar at Utti. The individual helicopter-maintenance schedule is determined by its flight hours and/or the time interval between work. On arrival, it is thoroughly checked over to assess its condition and identify any possible faults. The deepest maintenance levels require the whole helicopter to be completely taken apart and the components spread over the hangar floor. This process can take from two weeks to several months.

In January 2018, the Helicopter Battalion was divided into two companies that each operate a mix of NH-90s and MD500s supported by an Aircraft Maintenance Company. No. 1 Company is a high-readiness unit that specialises in all forms of special-operations training and tasks. No. 2 Company provides basic flight training from cadet level upwards for both the NH-90 and MD500 and operational and training support for Finland's other armed services and civil agencies. Finnish helicopters regularly participate in annual NATO special operation forces exercises, such as 'Night Hawk 2018' hosted in Denmark. Their participation involved 70 Utti Jaeger Regiment personnel and the Navy's Coastal Brigade plus three NH-90s, an MD500 and Finnish Navy RHIB as well as Zodiac vessels for use by combat divers and a special boat unit.

The first of a total of 12 MD500 light helicopters that first entered service in 1975 to train military helicopter pilots was followed by additional airframe purchases in 1982 and 1998. Today, seven remain in service, mainly used for a combination of pilot training and special operations missions. The helicopters were recently upgraded by a Patria programme that included the installation of a 'glass cockpit' with multifunction displays, making them fully compatible with night-vision equipment. New encrypted radio equipment and data links were also fitted, particularly with special operations tasks in mind.

Patria undertakes the major maintenance and modification work on Finland's NH-90 fleet at its modern facility on Utti airfield. (Patria/Johannes Wiehn)

Utti is also home to the NH-90 simulator facility. (Ilmavoimat)

The stunning sight of an NH-90 being serviced in a cold Arctic night under the glow of the Northern Lights. (Ilmavoimat)

A total of seven MD500Es remain in service, of which five are primarily used for training duties, and were recently upgraded to include a full night-vision capability. (Sami Niemeläinen)

Some Finnish MD500s are optimised for special forces' operations and regularly practise urban troop insertion techniques and assaults. (Puolustusvoimat)

Border Guard Service (Rajavartiolaitos)

Although regarded as a military organisation, the Rajavartiolaitos usually reports to the Ministry of the Interior, but on full mobilisation is incorporated into Finland's armed forces. It comprises around 3,800 personnel plus 500 conscripts. The reservists available can bring its mobilised strength up to around 12,600 personnel. Rajavartiolaitos work mainly involves border protection and some civil protection tasks.

The Border Guard service maintains an Air Patrol Squadron, which includes helicopters available on a 24-hour basis at three locations. These operate in search and rescue, medical transport, forest fire-fighting, environmental monitoring and any other assigned tasks. The service also has a 'Special Intervention Unit' that can be tasked to deal with emergency situations. The unit was created in 1992 primarily to deal with any situations resulting from the collapse of the Soviet Union. From the early 2000s, the cooperation between the 1st and 5th Border Guard Special Intervention Units, the Army's Utti Jaeger Regiment's Special Jaeger Battalion, the Navy Coastal Brigade's Special Operations Detachment, and the Police Rapid Response Unit has grown enormously. In a small country such as Finland, operators from all these special force units get to know each other well, with joint exercises used to refine cohesion and standardize operating methods.

The Air Patrol Squadron currently flies a total of 12 helicopters at any one time, made up of five H215 Super Pumas, five AB412s and four AW119 Koalas, plus two Dornier DO228 fixed-wing surveillance aircraft. Together they fly a combined total of around 4,000 flight hours each year. From its Helsinki-Vantaa airport base, the Rajavartiolaitos operates two of its H215 Super Pumas and two AW119s. The Rovaniemi airport base maintains three AB412s and two AW119s, with Turku Airport housing the two DO228s and three H215 Super Puma helicopters.

The Border Guard Service (Rajavartiolaitos) is tasked to protect Finland's land and maritime borders, operating two ageing DO228 aircraft and a number of helicopter types. (Rajavartiolaitos)

The two Border Guard DO228s, built in 1995, are based at Helsinki-Vantaa airport and used principally for maritime surveillance work. (Stefan Wright-Cole)

Right: Frequently tasked on rescue operations, Rajavartiolaitos helicopters like this H215 Super Puma have to be able to operate safely over all terrains and in all weathers. (Rajavartiolaitos)

Below: Two Rajavartiolaitos Air Patrol Squadron H215 Super Pumas are based at Helsinki-Vantaa and Turku Airports and often engage in sea rescue operations. Have dog, will travel, as a crew member and their German shepherd dog are winched down to a ferry as part of a ship-search operation. (Rajavartiolaitos)

Above: Rajavartiolaitos AB412EPs have proved versatile for all Air Patrol Squadron tasks. (Sami Niemeläinen)

Left: Members of the Border Guard Special Intervention Unit fast rope from an AB412 down to a Baltic ferry in a practice assault. (Rajavartiolaitos)

Four Agusta Westland AW-119 Koalas are flown by the Rajavartiolaitos and operated from bases at Rovaniemi and Helsinki-Vantaa. (Sami Niemeläinen)

In 2019, the Border Guard announced its 'MVX' programme to replace its two DO228 aircraft, which are experiencing increasing maintenance problems due to their age. The commitment was not a firm one, finance was an issue but an estimated 60M Euro was allocated for the programme. Following the 2022 Russian invasion of Ukraine, the Finnish Government decided to significantly increase that budget, to 163M Euro, for the purchase of a new multipurpose aircraft. The procurement decision is planned for 2023 with introduction to service by 2026. Candidates include a maritime variant of the Airbus CN295, Bombardier's Challenger 650 and versions of the ATR 42 and ATR 72.

Although having an avionics upgrade in 2016, in 2019 the 'MVX' programme was launched to identify a replacement and accelerated in 2022 after the Russian invasion of the Ukraine. (Sami Niemeläinen)

Chapter 9

From Neutral to NATO

T he signing of the Swedish and Finnish NATO accession documents on 5 July 2022 represented a seismic shift in both Finnish public and official attitudes, following the Russian invasion of Ukraine on 24 February 2022. Such a move would have been unimaginable even just a few months before. In reality, the Finnish Defence Forces had been quietly increasing their level of cooperation and integration with NATO member states within the EU framework and with the country's Nordic neighbours for some years. That process accelerated after the Russian occupation of Crimea in 2014, as Finland saw itself increasingly vulnerable to Vladimir Putin's revanchist Russia.

In 1994 Finland joined the Alliance's Partnership for Peace Programme and contributed to NATO's presences in Kosovo, Afghanistan, the Iraq-training mission and other operations.

Nordic Joint Training Exercises

Post-Cold War, Finland naturally looked to its Nordic neighbours to build collaborative contacts and enhance cooperation. Since 2014, the level of military cooperation has increased significantly, especially with its closest neighbour Sweden, to demonstrate their joint commitment to Baltic regional security. In 2015, following a formal agreement between their respective governments, co-operation between the Finnish and Swedish Air Forces (FISE) went much further.

The tri-national co-operation between Norway, Finland and Sweden has included the Arctic Challenge Exercises (ACE). Also, as part of Nordic Defence Cooperation (NORDEFCO) arrangements, the first ACE took place in 2013 in the far north of Scandinavia, where flight conditions are significantly less restrictive. The exercise takes place every second year; the most recent led by the Norwegian Air Force in 2021 and for that event Denmark contributed to the planning for the first time. From 7 to 18 June 2021 more than 3,000 personnel, 60 fighter and 10 support aircraft from Sweden, Finland, Norway, Denmark, Germany, the Netherlands, the UK and the US take part in the exercise. These included USAF F-16s from Spangdahlem, Germany, deployed to Sweden, 10 German Eurofighters to Rovaniemi Air Base, and participation by Norway's F-35s for the first time.

Since 2015, Swedish Gripens and Finnish F/A-18s have regularly participated in each other's major air defence exercise programmes. (Swedish Air Force)

In June 2021, an F/A-18 is prepared for its next sortie from its Rovaniemi base during NATO's Arctic Challenge Exercise 21 (ACE 21). (Ilmavoimat/ Joni Malkamäki)

Ten German Eurofighters flew missions from Rovaniemi for ACE 21, as part of NATO training to provide practice in planning and executing large composite air operations (COMAOs) and dissimilar air combat training. (Ilmavoimat/ Anne Torvinen)

Another avenue of cooperation has included regular training with the Norwegian Air Force through 'Arctic Fighter Meets' that have become a regular feature of cross-national training since 2015. Rovaniemi Air Base hosted 'Arctic Fighter Meet 21' (AFM 21) from 30 August to 3 September 2021. This saw Swedish Gripens from Kallax Air Base in Luleå, Norwegian F-16s from Bodø and Finland's F/A-18s and Hawk jet trainers all deployed to its most northerly main-operating base.

From 2016, joint Finnish-Swedish participation, each in the other's main air defence exercises each year, has become routine. As an example, for Finland's largest air defence exercise in 2021, 'Ruska 21,' from 4 to 9 October, 3,300 personnel were involved, and nearly half of them reservists. Following

In June 2021, for 'Arctic Fighter Meet 21' Norwegian F-16s from Bodø were deployed to Rovaniemi AB to operate alongside Swedish Gripens and Ilmavoimat F/A-18s and Hawks. (Ilmavoimat)

Finland's dispersed operations concept, as well as operating from the main bases at Rissala and Pirkkala, the F/A-18s of the defending forces also flew from Savonlinna, Varkaus, Kokkola-Pietarsaari, Seinäjoki and Kajaani airports and the Vieremä road base (separately known as Baana 21), Transport and liaison aircraft also flew from Pori during the exercise with adversary aircraft operating from Rovaniemi, Oulu and Luleå in Sweden. Around 50 aircraft participated, the majority being F/A-18s, plus Hawks, transport and liaison aircraft, an Army NH-90 helicopter and a Border Guard Dornier DO228 patrol aircraft. Ground-based air defence units operating at the Pirkkala Air Base and in the Lohtaja training area also took part.

Just a few weeks later, between 17 and 21 October 2021, for the Swedish air defence exercise 'Luftförsvarsövning (LFÖ) 21' the Finnish Air Force operated in both defensive and adversary air roles. Six F/A-18s were based at Såtenäs Air Base with Swedish Air Force Gripens as part of the defending forces, and three Hawks deployed to Visby on Gotland, to join the adversary operations. In addition to the aircraft fighter controllers, radar, command and control, support and logistics personnel also regularly take part in such activities.

'Ruska 21' was Finland's largest air defence exercise in 2021. It involved more than 50 Ilmavoimat, Border Guard and Swedish Air Force aircraft. (Ilmavoimat)

'Luftförsvarsövning (LFÖ) 21' was a major Swedish air-defence exercise with Gripens and Ilmavoimat F/A-18s operating alongside each other. (Swedish Armed Forces)

Solely Finnish military training exercises have their place too. Ilmataktiikka 22 was a live air exercise from 2 to 6 May 2022 in which all Finnish Air Force units were expected to participate. It involved approximately 24 F/A-18 Hornets, two Hawks plus transport and liaison aircraft. Rissala was the main operating base for the Hornets practising their air defence role, while Rovaniemi hosted the adversary aircraft. The main objective of the exercise was to train the fighter squadrons' Control and Reporting Centres under tactically challenging scenarios. These involved low-altitude sorties and supersonic flights well above 9,000m/30,000ft with aircraft using flares and chaff too.

Another form of cooperative training is often simply referred to as Cross Border Training (CBT). This is carried out just inside a country's airspace, or across borders, as a way of organising cost-effective training that benefits all. Those participating in CBT missions usually operate from their home

Rissala was the main operating base for 24 F/A-18s for Exercise Ilmataktiikka 22, a national Finnish training event. (Sami Niemeläinen)

Autumn colours predominate as an F/A-18C lands at Kupio AB during Exercise 'Ruska 22' that took place in early October 2022. (Sami Niemeläinen)

Autumn exercises are always at risk of snow, such as in late October 2018 at Rovaniemi Airbase during 'Trident Juncture'. (Ilmavoimat/ Minna Pyykönen)

bases, which saves on the logistics costs of the exercise. Typically, aircraft from Finland, Sweden and Norway fly in the missions, but, from time to time, participants from the air forces of other countries involved may be included. This might involve additional aircraft such as E-3s and Swedish airborne early-warning aircraft, and in-flight refuelling tankers.

Joint Exercises

As a NATO partner, Finland regularly takes part in Alliance-led exercises, with its participation significantly increased in recent years. This has included the Alliance-led Exercise 'Trident Junction 18', conceived in the post-2014 wake of Russia's occupation of Ukrainian Crimea. The exercise, centred on Norway from 25 October to 7 November 2018, and involved Finnish ground forces and nine Rovameni based F-18s. Flying from their home base and Norway's Ørland AB, the F-18s were supported by USAF KC-135R tankers from RAF Mildenhall. Finnish airfields have regularly hosted brief deployments of US combat aircraft since 2014.

Following vague Russian threats to Sweden and Finland after they announced their intention to join NATO, a number of bilateral and multilateral training deployments and exercises were rapidly put in place. These have seen short-term exercise deployments of US and British forces under names such as 'Vigilant Fox' and 'Vigilant Knife' as a way of developing cooperation further and as deterrent operations.

Air-refuelling support, often provided by USAF KC-135Rs, is now a regular part of exercises over Finland and for some Baltic air-policing missions. (USAFE)

In Spring 2016, Rissala AB hosted a squadron of F-15Cs from the Oregon Air National Guard, including this very colourful example. (Sami Niemeläinen)

In June 2021, it was the turn of the US Marine Corps VMFA-115 to take its F-18s to Kupoio where they worked alongside Ilmavoimat aircraft. (Sami Niemeläinen)

In August 2022, the USS Kearsarge was operating in the Baltic where its AV-8Bs took the opportunity to work with the Ilmavoimat's F/A-18s. (Ilmavoimat)

During AFM 21, three F/A-18s had the opportunity to air-refuel from a Luftwaffe A-400M in tanker configuration.

During 2022, a loose British-led multilateral arrangement, with origins in 2014, gained physical form in the immediate wake of Russia's invasion of Ukraine and has been used to facilitate a number of training exercises and temporary force deployments. Known as the Joint Expeditionary Force (JEF), it can bring together the rapid reaction capabilities of European military forces from Denmark, Estonia, Finland, Iceland, Latvia, Lithuania, the Netherlands, Norway and Sweden, able to act outside of NATO and EU frameworks if this is deemed necessary. Finland joined the JEF in 2017.

Between 6 and 17 June 2022, the RAF deployed four Typhoons from 6 Squadron and around 70 personnel to Rovaniemi AB for JEF training. The aircraft worked with Finnish AF F/A-18s and Swedish aircraft to bolster Finland's defence capability and to demonstrate partner nations' support following the Russian threats against the two countries following their announced intentions to join NATO. A similar RAF deployment, this time to Rissala AB from 28 to 30 June 2022, took place, this time with two F-35B fighters and around 60 personnel. Hosted by Karelia Air Command it gave Ilmavoimat F/A-18s an opportunity to briefly train with the British F-35s. Autumn 2022 brought the now-regular series of exercises when the Joutsa highway strip hosted Exercise 'Baana 22' from 25 to 30 September. Exercise 'Ruska 22' took place from 3 to 8 October, centred on Lapland Air Command and Rovaniemi and Tikkakosk Air Bases. The exercise involved around 3,700 personnel including 2,400 reservists and up to 50 aircraft, mostly F-18s, but also Hawks, NH-90s and PC-9NGs. External participation saw a Swedish Air Force JAS-39 Gripen detachment operate from Rovaniemi AB.

Giving physical form to the 'Joint Expeditionary Force' concept, four RAF Typhoons were deployed to Rovaniemi AB for training and a show of strength in June 2022. (Crown Copyright)

Two RAF F-35Bs were briefly hosted by Karelian Air Command in late June 2022, part of a hastily put together programme by JEF planners following unspecified Russian threats as Finland and Sweden made moves to join NATO. (Sami Niemeläinen)

From 25 to 30 September 2022, Exercise Baana 2022 saw the Joutsa road strip activated. (Ilmavoimat)

The following week, Exercise Ruska 22 saw this Finnish Hawk operating from Rissala AB and wearing special markings to celebrate 25 years of the Midnight Hawks. (Sami Niemeläinen)

Meanwhile, Swedish JAS-39 Gripens flew from Rovaniemi AB, operating in the air-defence role. (Ilmavoimat)

Even with significant cooperation with NATO's Baltic Air Policing mission, Finland's government had held to its neutral principles, a position unequivocally supported by the majority of its population. That support wavered slightly following the Russian occupation of Crimea in 2014, but changed radically in the immediate wake of the Russian invasion of Ukraine in 2022. Support for joining the Alliance shifted from just 19 percent in 2017 to 76 percent in May 2022, while that against NATO membership fell from 53 percent to just 12 percent. That directly led, just a few months later, to a seismic shift when Finland and Sweden signed NATO accession documents. Even prior to that signing, cooperation had quickly deepened, with Swedish and Finnish personnel attached to the NATO's Combined Air Operations Centre at Udem. At the same time US, British and other NATO forces had deployed to Finland for training exercises, as a show of strength and an indicator of solidarity.

Following eventual formal ratification of Finnish and Swedish accession to NATO still pending in November 2022, the two states will bring significant extra military capability to the Alliance. This is particularly important to Northern Europe, which is regarded as vulnerable to any potential future Russian aggression. Positions will be created in the Alliance command structure for Finnish and Swedish personnel, coupled with a realignment of those command structures to accommodate the two new members. Both countries will become full participants in NATO training and exercise programmes. Finland, in particular, is likely to host many of these events, given its long land border with a hostile Russia, which has continued to threaten unspecified responses to its NATO membership.

A modern and capable Air Force, Finland's concept of 'total defence' is reliant on the country's small core of highly competent professionals, who are ably supported by a large pool of well-trained and well-equipped conscripts and reservists. These strengths are clearly reflected in the Ilmavoimat's motto of Qualitas Potentia Nostra (Quality is Our Strength).

(Ilmavoimat)

Other books you might like:

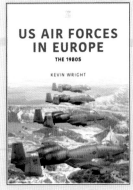

Air Force Series,
Vol. 4

Airline Series,
Vol. 2

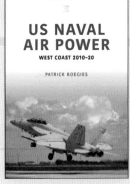

Air Forces Series,
Vol. 2

Air Forces Series,
Vol. 3

Air Forces Series,
Vol. 1

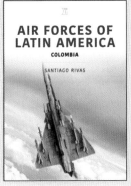

Air Forces Series,
Vol. 5

For our full range of titles please visit:
shop.keypublishing.com/books